LOVE
Never Ends

PAT MONAHAN

Copyright © 2020 by Pat Monahan

ISBN   Softcover   978-1-951469-72-6

All rights reserved. No part of this book may be reproduced or transmitted in any form or by any means, electronic or mechanical, including photocopying, recording, or by any information storage and retrieval system without express written permission from the author, except in the case of brief quotations embodied in critical reviews and certain other non-commercial uses permitted by copyright law.

Printed in the United States of America.

To order additional copies of this book, contact:
Bookwhip
1-855-339-3589
https://www.bookwhip.com

Contents

Dedication v

Acknowledgments vii

Chapter 1   Tommy 1

Chapter 2   Faith 5

Chapter 3   Tommy's Blessings 8

Chapter 4   The Eagle 16

Chapter 5   The Bench 20

Chapter 6   Going Home 25

Chapter 7   The Shark 30

Chapter 8   Reflections 33

About the Author 41

Dedication

I dedicate this book to my precious
grandson Tommy Monahan who died so young,
yet who continues to teach and love us........................

from heaven.

ACKNOWLEDGMENTS

The Holy Spirit has always been the most important source of guidance for me as long as I can remember. As you will note I am not a professional writer. However, it is the Holy Spirit who answers my prayers for the most effective words to express myself.

I thank my husband Tom for his patience during those long hours I sat at my computer requesting not to be disturbed. I promise the reservations for dinner will be less often now.

I thank my seven year old grandson Connor for creating my book cover with his artistic abilities. He never met Tommy, but he knows Tommy's spirit and Connor is a great example of love.

Many thanks go to my daughter Melissa Connolly for her patience and trips to Staten Island to help me with this book. Melissa taught me how to be more proficient with the computer in order to prepare my manuscript for the publisher. She dropped whatever she had to do and ran in a minute's notice. This book would not exist without her help.

I am forever grateful to my son Tom and his wife Maria for always being there to share their stories about Tommy. Tommy would not forgive me if I didn't thank their dogs Molly and Mac. Whenever I arrive at their house Molly and Mac are greeting me as soon as I get out of my car with their perky voices. As I walk through their door they smother me with their love and kisses. I believe Tommy has something to do with that!

I thank everyone that has allowed me to enter their grieving souls to share with them some things I know about bereavement. I know and appreciate your ability to trust a stranger with your deep pain. May you all find the peace that comes with dealing with the stages of grief as you struggle to get to the other side, coming to ACCEPTANCE and GRATITUDE for your loved one's lives as well as their signs.

Chapter 1

"I am the Resurrection and the life; those who
believe in me, though they die, will live; and everyone
who lives and believes in Me will live; and everyone who lives
and believes in Me will never die"
John 11:25-26

My husband and I will never forget the moment we were told that our son Tom's house was on fire around 11 p.m. on December 16, 2007. I began praying to the Blessed Mother, pleading with her to keep our family safe. My heart sank as we approached their house, having difficulty parking our car due to the fire truck and police cars near the house.

As my husband and I approached the house the firemen were still attending to the effects of the fire, securing the safety of the house following the destruction from the fire. The front door was open. Although there were no lights on we noticed the oak foyer staircase no longer existed, yet was still smoldering. All the windows of the house were broken and smoke was everywhere.

We told the firemen who we were and they informed us "One man was taken to Staten Island Hospital North and a little boy was taken to

Staten Island Hospital South". At that time we assumed the man was our son. Out of our minds with fear, we knew our son would want us to go to his son. Fortunately, a policeman offered to escort our car to the hospital to be with our nine year old grandson Tommy as soon as possible.

Driving to the hospital in a state of shock I forgot the faithful words of the Hail Mary. I knew the Blessed Mother heard my plea although I could only say, "Dear Mary please help our grandson, please be with him and take care of him".

When we reached the hospital we saw our sons Tom and Craig standing outside Tommy's cubicle with the curtain closed. At that moment I knew my son Tom was not at the other hospital. I also felt God's presence and was reassured the Blessed Mother was with Tommy.

The man that was taken to the other hospital was a young man who lived across the street from our family's house. Bobby Ryan was on the phone with his girl friend at the time; Tommy's oldest sister Ashley. Ashley was away at college. Bobby saw the smoke and went running across the street to get the family out of the house. He broke the window of the kitchen door with his arm that ended up needing stitches.

Back at the hospital with my family, the doctor's allowed me to be at Tommy's side following the request of our son Tom. I looked at my grandson's face and knew Mary was with him because his face looked as though he was only sleeping. There were no signs of stress regardless of the attempts to revive him whenever his heart stopped beating. As I approached him I talked softly, yet clearly to him, "Tommy, Grandma and Grandpa are here with you now. We are with Dad and Uncle Craig. We will not leave you for a minute. We know you must be frightened, but we are convinced you are in excellent hands and we will make sure you get everything you need. I love you so much and I am so proud of who you are. I will never leave your side, no matter what." I continued "Tommy, I want you to feel all the healing energy that surrounds you. The energy is so peaceful and serene. As you breathe in feel the healing energy come into your body and blow out all the crap that is inside you."

I kept reminding him who was there, "Dad, Grandpa and Uncle Craig are still with us. I love you so much. All the angels and saints are also here to protect and keep you safe. I love you so much". Tommy died with a smile on his face. I believe the Blessed Mother carried him to heaven.

We certainly were not prepared to lose such a beautiful, vibrant grandson to death. If possible we all would have done anything God had asked of us to save this precious and very gifted boy. Yet, I believe Tommy already accomplished on this earth what he came here for. His soul was ready to reap the rewards God promises us.

I do find comfort knowing Tommy will never know the pain of losing a loved one to death, he will never feel the rejection of a girl or have to take another written test. He now only knows the love of Jesus and the Blessed Mother as he sees the love that comes from all of us. He can now be with any creature he loved when he was here on earth. I believe he is humbled and touched by the numerous ways he is being remembered and memorialized by others

Interestingly enough, Tommy continues to serve the Lord from heaven. I write this book hoping to help others see the signs we get from our loved ones who have died. The signs Tommy sends us are the gifts God gives him.

Some Staten Islander's know him as Tommy Monahan, the extraordinary 9 year old animal lover who lives in heaven with his dog Sophie. Their job is to welcome all the animals that cross over the Rainbow Bridge into heaven.

The Native Americans know him as "one of the enlightened ones." His Earth Camp friends know him as "Steve Irwin Jr." and the neighbors know him as "the boy who loves and protects all creatures great and small."

"Tommy is my grandson whose spirit comes to us in various forms, reminding us that he continues to watch over us until we meet again in heaven. His spiritual presence to us on a frequent basis is evidence of ever-lasting life. Death does not mean life has ended."

I wrote my first book, "To Thee We Do Cry" (A Grandmother's Journey Through Grief), to share the effects Tommy's life and death had on the lives of everyone who knew him. He died on Dec. 17, 2007. The incredible soul that we know as Tommy Monahan continues to affect those of us who love and miss his physical presence on earth.

I want to share the many events that have occurred since his death; a reminder of his spiritual presence with us! It is also my intent to prove to the skeptics who suffer the death of their loved ones; that their loved one's spirits remain with them. The bereaved just need to open their minds and hearts; believe their loved ones are waiting to hear from them; and watch and listen for the signs they send them. They are out there! I believe that God gives their spirits the Grace to show up.

However, everyone needs to be careful not to ask for a specific sign. You need to be open for all possibilities. You need to be patient, without anger….and believe.

CHAPTER 2

"Whoever follows me will have the light of my
life and will never walk in darkness"
John 8:12

On my 79th birthday our son Scott presented me with a beautiful tapestry of Our Lady of Guadalupe with a rod to hang it on my wall. Scott had the tapestry blessed by his parish priest Father Fernando Lopez from Saint Agnes Church in Atlantic Highlands. My son and his son Scott hung the tapestry on our wall that has pictures of our seven children as babies. The tapestry hangs over a small bookcase filled with brochures that I use as a Bereavement Minister to help the bereaved with their pain. Baby pictures of our nineteen grandchildren sit on top of the bookcase with a guardian angel night-light watching over the young boys and girls.

My daily prayers always begin and end with the guardian angel prayer and the rosary at some point during the day. I've always been devoted to the Blessed Mother. Receiving the gift of this tapestry between my birthday and our 60th wedding anniversary is a clear reminder of God's graces.

Scott reminded me of the miracle experienced by Juan Diego on his way to Mass in Mexico on Dec. 9, 1531. The sighting and message from the Blessed Mother on that hill at Tepeyac are evidence of the signs God sends us at significant times. My faith reminds me of the first miracle at Cana when Jesus responded to His mother's request when He turned the water into wine. These miracles are signs of God's love for us. Through Jesus' love and devotion to His mother we understand why Mary has been called to help so many who are devoted to her son. We are drawn to her gentleness and strength in doing God's will. I am so grateful that Jesus sacrificed Himself through the crucifixion so we can have ever-lasting life. At the same time He gives the deceased the gifts to show their spirits in so many different ways. Hopefully you will be enlightened to your own connections.

Grandpa, Tommy & Grandma

Chapter 3

Tommy's Blessings

In August 2010, two days before my contract was to be signed with I Universe to publish the 1st edition of "To Thee We Do Cry", I was filled with anxiety. I began questioning my decision to publish Tommy's story. I was concerned about the public's possible reactions to this tragic event. I was specifically concerned about questions or feedback Tommy's parents and siblings might be faced with. I couldn't sleep that night worrying about his family having to re-live that time if approached by others. I prayed hard all night. I asked The Holy Spirit to guide me in a way I could alleviate any doubts or accept the book may not be good. I asked the Blessed Mother to show me what this mother should do.

The following day I drove to New Jersey from Staten Island to watch Tommy's younger sister Gabrielle play on her travel soccer team. When the game ended, as we were headed for our cars, I expressed my trepidations to my son Tom and his wife Maria. Both of them reassured me they would support any efforts that could keep their son's memory alive.

I drove home from New Jersey a little less anxious, yet remained uncomfortable. That night while saying my prayers I called upon my grandson's spirit saying, "Tommy I need you to show me a sign. Do I publish this book or not? I don't want the book to have an adverse effect on your family. Unfortunately, I need a sign before I speak to the publisher tomorrow." No one knew about my prayer to Tommy.

While eating breakfast with my husband that next morning our son Tom stopped by. I offered to make him breakfast. He looked at me with a serious tone in his voice and said, "No thanks, I'm here on a mission. Tommy sent me. While I was sitting on my front steps this morning, talking to Tommy I was looking into the clover in my front yard. I spotted a four-leaf clover and as I bent down to pick it up, I heard a voice in my head say 'This is for Grandma'." My son gently dug up the root of this clover and carefully removed the dirt from the root. He knew this was a special assignment! He took a 3"x5" piece of white paper, made a pin hole in the paper and carefully placed the root through the hole. He then smoothed the leaf flat onto the paper, and came to our house to complete his mission.

He reverently placed the beautiful gift into the palm of my hand while the tears slowly filled my eyes. All I could say was "Thank you Tom. You have no idea how much this means to me. Really, you don't understand the meaning of this precious gift. I love it beyond words. You just don't know! This is the sign I asked Tommy for last night. I don't believe this! Thank you, thank you my beautiful grandson! I love you so much! Thank you God for this gift, for answering my prayers!" This clover sits in a frame next to his picture.

According to Irish tradition, those who find a four-leaf clover are destined for good-luck, as each leaf in the clover symbolizes good measure. To me the four leaves represent the cross as we say "The Father, the Son and the Holy Spirit."

As a result of this experience I knew I needed to put the four-leaf clover in my book. After all, this is Tommy's blessing of my book. Our daughter Terry Quercia was the computer expert that e-mailed my manuscript to the publisher. Terry created a four-leaf clover for us to have placed in the book as a sign of Tommy's blessing. We put one clover on the spine of the book and three together at the end of each chapter. Three of them together represent The Father, The Son and The Holy Spirit. This book would not happen without my faith.

On the day I finished writing my first book I had an experience I would like to share with you. My last page was written approximately 3 pm. When I picked up my paper to review what I had written, the sun was shining brightly through the window over my kitchen table where I was sitting. As I read my final words the tears just flowed from my eyes. I was overcome with emotion as my hands began to tremble. I sensed Tommy's presence. I took a few deep breaths to settle down.

I gently placed my paper onto the table with my left hand and the pen a few inches to the right of the paper. I experienced mixed emotions; relief, gratitude, some sadness and anxiety. I talked to Tommy, telling him I hoped he liked my book and how much I loved him. Through my tears I noticed a lightning bug crawl out from under the paper.

I knew the bug was Tommy. I have never seen a lightning bug in broad daylight, and certainly never in my house before. He stopped crawling when he reached my pen. While continuing to talk to him he did not move. I told him I knew he was letting me know he was here with me on this journey, hopefully with approval. Tears continued as I picked him up with a tissue, explaining how he would be happier outside with his friends since there were no children to play with in here.

I took him onto our back deck and opened the tissue as I continued speaking to him. When he initially did not fly away, I told him he would always be in my heart. I assured him that finishing my book did not mean that I would stop talking to him on a daily basis. I hoped that he would always feel my love. I encouraged him to have fun with his friends. Then he flew away, turned around, landing on my right shoulder. I reminded him my love would be there forever. He then flew off my shoulder and landed on my glass back door that leads to my kitchen. I laughed and smiling said, "Thanks Tommy. I believe you are telling me you will always watch over me. Feel my hugs and kisses sweetheart, I love you now and forever."

Speaking of bugs, I am so grateful our grandson John shared so many of Tommy's interests; i.e. all types of bugs and animals great and small, exploring nature and the environment including fishing, camping, collecting bird's feathers, rocks, stones and archeological artifacts. John thinks of Tommy often even though he was only five years old when Tommy died. When I began writing my first book John drew a picture of Tommy and Sophie inside a heart to be printed in my first book.

John was so grateful and proud to be able to participate in the Earth Camp that Tommy attended the last few years of his life. John loved learning all that the camp offered and believes Tommy was with him during those excursions. John was considered an expert by many of the campers because he knew so much about their findings. He found artifacts the counselor's didn't see. John believed Tommy pointed him in the right directions for his precious findings.

Tommy   Earth Camp   John

Tommy's cousins Craig and Christian enjoy Tommy's visits with them. They were only five and three years old when Tommy died. However, they were as close to Tommy as brothers. They lived next door to Tommy and he was in their yard and house all the time. They were his little brothers. Since he died they feel his presence through the multitude of animals and birds that inhabit their back yard. The night before what would have been Tommy's 21st ^{birthday} Uncle Craig was sitting on his front porch in the dark. He heard "WHOO, WHOO, WHOO...... WHOO". He thought his neighbor was playing a joke on him. However, again he heard "WHOO, WHOO, WHOO.... WHOO". He went off the porch quietly and spotted an owl perched on the turret in front of his son Craig's bedroom window. We think Tommy spirit came to his cousin to wish him a "Happy Birthday". There are only three days between their birthdays. WHOOO knows?

Our son Craig came over one morning about 8 years ago, to show us a video-tape he had taken in his back yard. He and his boys Craig and Christian decided to capture the moment for others to witness. The boys were in the house with him at the time. From their kitchen window he began taping two young squirrels playing with each other. Out of the corner of his eye, he detected movement on the swing set. He pointed his camera that way and, sure enough the middle of the three swings was swaying back and forth; a scene he and the boys often witnessed. The middle swing is a toddler's swing with a safety bar across the front.

All of a sudden, as it swayed back and forth, one of the squirrels leaped up and into the swing. He put his front paws on the bar and enjoyed riding the swing to and fro for a few moments before jumping down. What a sight to see and validating to Tommy's cousins. They have evidence that Tommy's spirit is hanging out in their yard, just as they thought. Young Craig said, "That was Tommy's favorite swing."

Only seven years old now, their youngest brother Connor never met Tommy, however he knows his cousin's spirit comes to them through the animals. When Connor's parents were awaiting his birth they reviewed their long list of names. One of the names Uncle Craig considered naming their son was Wolf in memory of Tommy. Aunt Sharin wasn't having that! She went searching on-line and learned Connor means "little wolf". There you go! Problem solved! His name is Connor Thomas and Tommy's parents are his godparents.

When Grandpa and I went to the nursery to see Connor right after he was born, we became very emotional. We have 19 grandchildren. The only two babies born with red hair are Tommy and Connor. Both babies had the same shaped head with similar faces. Don't get me wrong, no one believed Connor was Tommy re-incarnated. However, we do believe Tommy's spirit had a relationship with Connor in-vitro.

We also believe Tommy came through Connor to let us know he will watch over Connor. It turns out as a baby Connor always had a big smile on his face and was often found laughing heartily while starring into space. As humorous as Tommy could be, we believe Tommy was playing with Connor during those earlier months.

I'll never forget the day I was baby-sitting for Connor when he was 18 months old. He was having a moment. So I distracted him by saying, "Connor, look out the kitchen door at the squirrel on the deck!" Connor ran over to the door and said, "I know grandma. That's Tommy! He visits us." Out of the mouths of babes!

Our daughter Terry and her family live in Ohio. They stayed at our house during Christmas week last year. They slept in the large bedroom we call "the grandchildren's room". Uncle Craig built it for the youngsters' sleepovers when they were young. Tommy's cousin Joey was sleeping in that room with his parents last year. Everyone was sound asleep when all of a sudden they were awakened by music. They realized the music was coming from the lap-top that had been turned off and placed on a dresser across the room from their beds. When Terry went to retrieve her lap-top she realized home movies from a DVD in the lap-top was where the music was coming from. As weird as that was, they all believed Tommy was playing games with Joey during his sleepover after all these years! Comforted by Tommy's spirit's presence they all went back to sleep.

Grandmas Sleepovers with Tommy, Ryan, Joseph, Russell, Kevin, Thomas, Scottie

Family Vacation: Kayla, Christina, Joseph, Scottie, Kathleen, Tommy, Gabrielle

Beavais Hudson American Legion Post Color Corps. Memorial Day Ceremony

Vice Commander Grandpa, Craig, Tommy, Gabrielle Christian, Uncle Craig

CHAPTER 4

The Eagle

Tommy loved learning about the Native Americans and their culture. The biggest poster in his bedroom was a Native Chief. He practiced some of their traditions, such as scraping the corn off the cobs that hung on their front door in the autumn. He would place the corn in his lizard's water dish and leave it in the yard for the birds to feed on. Tommy's Mom Maria gave me a book she reads that has a paragraph I am happy to share with you, explaining the Native's understanding of an eagle.

The book is titled "Spirits of the Earth", by Bobby Lake-Thom. Bobby tells us, "Eagles are always very special and good signs. They represent protection, wealth, wisdom, foresight, strength, and spirituality. If one or more should approach while you are praying or performing a ceremony, then you know your prayers have been answered. If I see an Eagle sitting in a tree, on a telephone pole, or alongside the road while I am traveling, I know it is telling me that I will encounter a spiritual person up ahead, such as a medicine man or a ceremonial leader. Or if I am planning or performing a ceremony somewhere and the Eagle comes in I know that it will be a good group of people and a good ceremony. Sometimes the Great Creator sends an Eagle just to check up on us, so when we see this, we always give special thanks to the Creator and the

Eagle. The Eagle carries our prayers directly to the Great Creator." This information is so pertinent to my story!

Eagle sightings on Staten Island were very rare and almost non-existent in 2012. However, on August 25 that summer our son Tom was sitting on the front steps of their new home, one block from Prince Bay Beach. Tom was talking to his son's spirit when he spotted an Eagle perched in a tree 300 ft. from their house. He alerted Maria and ran for their high-powered binoculars to get a closer view of this regal bird-of-prey. They were able to clearly see his eyes open and close and marveled at the ruffling of his soft feathers each time he turned his head. They could not believe he stayed there so long. They felt Tommy's spirit and believed Tommy was demonstrating his power; coming to Mom and Dad as the creature that is closest to heaven.

Cell phone in hand, Tom phoned to tell us this exciting news. He had to leave a message on our phone since we were at daily Mass. The moment I picked up our message we flew by car to the beach. In the meantime Tom had called his brother Craig who brought his two young sons Craig and Christian down to the beach and they saw their cousin Tommy's spirit as an Eagle. When we arrived the Eagle had flown down the embankment onto a piling in the water of the bay. He remained on that piling long enough for us to thank him for coming to us in such a glorious way. He then proceeded to fly away and I yelled to him "We love you sweetheart!".

I told our son "Tommy showed up today to remind us his birthday is coming." I was grateful for this gift from God just days before his birthday. As days passed, Tom and Maria saw the Eagle return to their home often, with the same routine.

Sometime in September weeks had gone by without seeing the Eagle. They assumed he flew south for the winter. However, on October 13, 2012 Gabrielle came running into their house with great excitement, "Tommy's back!" It was during an intimate house party to celebrate her Confirmation. We all went rushing outside to witness the most unusual demonstration of love.

At first the Eagle was flying directly over their house. Then he went across the street, over the rooftop of that facility. Tommy's spirit flew back and forth for a good 5 minutes. It was a glorious sight to behold! His wing span went on forever. He tipped his wings back and forth as if he was saying, "Hello family! Can you see me now? This is my confirmation gift to you Gabrielle. Congratulations!" We were watching a private nature show.

When the Eagle flew to that piling in the water close to the beach, the kids all ran down to the beach to witness him a bit closer. They watched until he flew out over the bay. Tommy's dad took the children for a clean-up walk along the beach in memory of Tommy; an act father and son often did together. Since our daughter Terry was wearing high heels in the sand, she chose to walk back to the house. On her way back she spotted a piece of paper in the wet sand and bent down to pick it up. She noticed it was a washed –up prayer card that was wrinkled. She looked at it carefully and saw it written in Latin. The back of the card was a picture of Padre Pio.

Padre Pio was born Francesco Fergione on May 25, 1887 in Italy and died Sept. 23,1968. His parents were peasant farmers who were illiterate. However, they narrated bible stories to their children. Francesco was very religious. His mother said he was able to speak with Jesus, Mary and his guardian angels as a young child and assumed that everyone else could do so.

Ordained a Capuchin Franciscan priest he took the simple vows of poverty, chastity and obedience. On September 20, 1918, while hearing confessions, Padre Pio had his first occurrence of the stigmata: bodily marks, pain and bleeding in locations corresponding to the crucifixion wounds of Jesus. This continued for fifty years until the end of his life.

Those close to him attest that he began to manifest several spiritual gifts, including the gifts of healing, bi-locations, levitation, prophecy and miracles. At the time of his death his body appeared unwounded, with no sign of scarring. Saint Padre Pio of Pietrelcina was beatified and canonized in 2002 by Pope John Paul II.

When Terry found Padre Pio's card in the sand, she had tears in her eyes. Earlier that year she was in Italy at the Vatican and brought Gabrielle a crucifix necklace blessed by the Pope. She was Gabrielle's sponsor for her Confirmation. She believed this prayer card was another gift from Tommy and gave it to Gabrielle when they returned to the house.

I believe that card was another sign of everlasting life. After all, Padre Pio's stigmata reminds us of the crucifixion, and Jesus died so we could have life everlasting.

I couldn't believe my foolishness in church earlier in the day. Sitting in the church pew, waiting for the Confirmation ceremony to begin, I was missing Tommy terribly. I tried to subdue my tears, but my body was trembling. Our son Craig was sitting next to me. He said, "Mom what's wrong?" I replied, "I miss Tommy. He never made his Confirmation". Craig put his arm around me saying, "Mom, Tommy didn't need to make his Confirmation. He's in heaven, and besides this is Gabrielle's day." I said, "You're right Craig. Thanks!" Little did I know at that time, what was to happen that afternoon when Tommy showed up, reminding us he continues to be with us in a special way. God is good!

The Staten Island Advance (a local newspaper) printed an article in the newspaper announcing the sightings of Eagles and their nest along the shoreline not far from the house our family lived in until they moved back where Tommy and Gabrielle lived before the fire. On December 4, 2012 I dreamt that Tommy came to us as a golden Eagle.

Now Tommy's parents live in the house that my parents lived in for over 40 years. Craig built his own house on the property next to Tommy and his family. Their houses are approximately one mile from the beach. As I write this chapter during the summer of 2019, I am reminded that an Eagle flew over their homes this spring. The day my son spotted the Eagle we were convinced it was Tommy. Was he checking out his old neighborhood, letting us know he is still keeping his eye on us?

Chapter 5

The Bench

Prior to Tommy's death there were many days Tommy's dad would be greeted by his son when he returned from work, requesting his dad bring him back to the various sites Tommy had been that day with his Earth Camp friends. They often ended up at Lemon Creek to explore nature's gifts. That was where Tommy learned from his dad how to safely hold the horseshoe crabs, use a sea shell to remove the parasites off the underbelly of the crabs, returning them safely to the bay. The Park Rangers knew Tommy well and made him an Honorary Park Ranger after witnessing his knowledge and sensitivity with all of nature's creatures.

N.Y. State Senator Andrew Lanza's office made arrangements for a bench to be placed on this spot in Tommy's name. Senator Lanza learned about Tommy's efforts to save the horseshoe crabs that entered the lagoon at high tide and getting caught amongst the rocks when the tide receded.

Senator Lanza stated that "a small fish in a big pond was deserving of attention." It rained the day of the dedication of the bench. It was a bitter-sweet day. The rain reminded us that the angels were crying for the pain we have while coping with Tommy's death. The dedication of the bench was to be a living reminder of all the joy Tommy experienced at this site while he was saving the horseshoe crabs, fishing with his dad, grandpa, Uncle Craig, sister Gabrielle and cousins, exploring nature's wonders or just cleaning up the litter left by others.

When the bench was placed at Lemon Creek, their house was close to the beach, and had a great view from the 2nd floor. You can see Tommy's bench from their 2nd floor bedroom window. This bench is in front of the lagoon at the beach where Lemon Creek enters into the Raritan Bay.

There is a small wooden bridge that crosses over the entrance to the lagoon. Sitting on the bench you face the large rocks on the edge of the bulkhead of the creek. The view is magnificent! You look out over the bay watching the small boats channel in and out of the entrance to the marina. As the boats leave the marina you can see their red navigation lights. As they enter the marina you can see their green navigation lights. Sitting on his bench you can look along the shoreline at the neighborhood Tommy's family lived at while their home was being renovated following the fire. In the distance you see the church steeple at Mt. Loretto.

In 1882 Father John Drumgoole founded The Mission of the Immaculate Conception (popularly known as Mt. Loretto). This was an orphanage for boys and girls, one of the largest child-care institutions in the country. The children helped work on the farm when not in school. When I was a teenager I would take some of the young children into town on Saturdays to buy them some candy.

Mt. Loretto is run by Catholic Charities. They offer many services for the disabled and handicapped people of all ages. Carl's Recovery Center is there for anyone struggling with addiction. A Friendship Club for senior citizens opens 5 days a week with comprehensive resources for seniors.

Today, while sitting on Tommy's bench, looking at the glorious view, you can hear the seagulls and purple martins flying to and from their protected birdhouses nearby. The purple martins are an endangered species of birds that fly to Brazil during the winter and return to North America in the spring, arriving at their breeding ground at Lemon Creek in April. Their colony of bird houses are protected and maintained by Gloria Depp and the Nature Section of the Staten Island Institute of Arts and Sciences.

One of my Bereavement Groups had a memorial service at Tommy's bench for their deceased loved ones during one of our meeting nights. It turns out, while reading a prayer I had written to begin our ceremony at the bench, I heard a bird whistling. I quietly believed it was my grandson reminding me he was with us. Once the prayer ended Rita said. "Pat that bird was your grandson behind you on a tree branch!"

Lucille brought small wooden coasters made from tree branches. Our group wrote messages on the coasters. They wanted to throw them into the bay for their loved ones. When I tossed my wood chip with Tommy's name on it into the bay, the tide sent the wood chip under the bridge, into the lagoon. We all watched it come out from under the bridge and what do you think we saw? A beautifully healthy-looking horseshoe crab followed the chip into the lagoon. We all were so excited to see such evidence of my grandson. Each group member was amazed when we witnessed all their wood chips ended up together in the lagoon, despite the different directions they had sent their chips when they threw there's into the bay.

This group's session was on Spirituality. Everyone experienced a spiritual message; the deceased are clearly with us even though their body no longer is with us! The group members were filled with gratitude for their experience that night. That evening I couldn't stop thanking Tommy for showing up and my prayers of gratitude to the Lord for allowing Tommy to come to us!

Following the service Roberta looked out over the bay and announced, "Tommy's here. Look at that ship going by! The only letters on the tanker are a huge letter T. He's letting us know he's here with us!" I yelled, "Hi Tommy! Thanks for showing up again".

Once you sit on Tommy's bench you don't want to leave that spot. Occasionally you can see the big ships passing through the channel close by. At times you may hear the ships sound their whistle when they are about to pass another ship. Tommy's bench gets lots of use. Most times we go there we will see people sitting there eating lunch, relaxing and enjoying the view, resting during their long walks through the park, mother's feeding their children in the stroller and some folks reading their books. When Gabrielle is home from college she and her friends often end up at the bench after their long runs.

Lemon Creek with Joseph, Tommy, Ryan, Craig

Tommy and Joseph's catch of the day

Lemon Creek

Dad and Tommy fishing with the bamboo pole Grandpa made

CHAPTER 6

Going Home

Although there were many changes in the house due to the renovations after the fire, moving back was a difficult decision for Maria. However, this was the only home Gabrielle knew when her brother was still with her. She also missed her neighborhood friends.

Gabrielle was entering the High School only blocks from the Princewood Ave. house. She was going to play soccer for Tottenville High School. Maria became very involved with the girls' soccer team, almost like a team mom. Mom realized that living close to the school would make life easier for her daughter.

Therefore, the family returned "home". The first day that dad went to work and Gabrielle left for school, Maria stood in her kitchen doorway looking out into the backyard. She began questioning her decision about returning to Princewood Ave.

Thinking about her son Tommy, she asked him if she made the right choice. Immediately the light above her head blinked on and off. The entire house had been re-wired. That light was connected to the lights on the kitchen ceiling. However, the only light that went on was the one over her head. Maria said, "Is that you Tommy?" Again, only the light above her head blinked on and off.

A feeling of peace and acceptance came over Maria. Mom was so relieved and reassured of her choice to return home. I was so thrilled for her when she called to share this experience with me.

As time goes by the family continues to get many signs from Tommy that assure them he is happy they are back home.

On Christmas Eve morning in 2017 my son Tom was not feeling the spirit of Christmas. December is a difficult month with the anniversary of Tommy's death so close to Christmas. Unless you have lost a child to death you cannot understand the intense pain a parent feels as Christmas approaches.

Tom began pruning close to the house since the weather was unseasonably warm. The ivy was climbing under the siding of the house. He struggled, bending over, cutting those very tangled vines from the house. Tugging away at them, he found shards of glass from the broken windows during the day of the fire. While carefully removing the glass, Tom spotted what appeared to be green ribbon or tape from a postal-service paper stuck in the dirt. It felt like a hard piece of plastic stuck in the ground.

Covered in vines, he scratched away the dirt that was covering a 3" plastic Christmas bear with a tiny baby bear on its shoulder. The body of the bear was a green Christmas tree. My son became emotional as he felt his son's presence. This mama and baby bear was a Christmas gift to his dad, from his son. I lived in that house with my parents and siblings from 1956 until I married. Tom and Maria bought that house from my dad. None of us has ever seen this Christmas bear. God is good!

Tommy's younger sister Gabrielle is in college now. She and her friends often take long runs on and off the campus grounds. One day she was running alone and winding down in the town outside the college. She spotted an elderly man who was struggling with the packages he had in his hand. Although she was headed in the opposite direction, she approached him saying, "Excuse me sir. Can I help you? I can carry those if you are headed for the bus."

The man responded, "Yes thank you. I don't recognize you. I know everyone in town. Where are you from?" Gabrielle said, "I go to the college and often run through town when I work out." He asked, "What's your name?" When she told him her name was Gabrielle he began to cry and said, "I can't believe this. My daughter Gabrielle died many years ago and today is her birthday. This morning I was feeling so sad and asked her to send me a sign. She sent you to me. You are my angel today. Thank you so much for your kindness."

Tommy had a very close relationship with his oldest sister Ashley. Ashley was like his younger Mom. They loved each other dearly. Ashley was in her college dorm the night of the fire. Distraught over his sudden death, Ashley and her boyfriend at that time, went to see a medium approximately one month after Tommy died.

The medium told Ashley that her brother was showing her a rabbit. The rabbit had no meaning to Ashley at that time. However, while driving home from the session Ashley and her boyfriend were stopped at a red light in their neighborhood. (Keep in mind this is in the middle of winter in NYC. We will never see a rabbit in January.)

All of a sudden a rabbit crossed the street directly in front of their car. They were elated, "There's Tommy's rabbit"! Ashley received a message from her brother. That was over 11 years ago. Life moves on for all of us, but the love Tommy shares with all of us never ends. Ashley works for the ASPCA, met and fell in love with the perfect man of her dreams, Matt. The day I am writing this chapter happens to be Ashley & Matt's 1st Wedding Anniversary. Their adorable shelter-rescued dog Bruiser was their ring bearer at their very personal and intimate wedding ceremony. At the ceremony as Bruiser came down the aisle with their rings, I could feel Tommy's spirit with him. This month the three of them will be moving into their first house, directly across the street from the house Ashley, Tommy and their family lived before the fire.

This past Mother's Day my son Tom saw a rabbit in their back yard. He also found two four-leafed clovers that he gave to Ashley for their new home. That day Ashley told them she was pregnant. Although this was an unplanned pregnancy since they were consumed with all the work getting into their new home, they were happy to share the news. Ashley realized the baby was conceived on her mother Maria's birthday. Therefore, she believed this baby was also a gift from Tommy for their Mom on Mother's Day. Hearing this news brought tears to my eyes. I was amazed about the connections to the rabbit. They are prolific. Years ago was Tommy telling his sister he would send them this baby?

As it turns out, I had our anniversary card for Ashley and Matt sealed before this date, ready to bring to the couple. On the envelope I placed a sticker of a butterfly approaching a floral bush. On the back of the envelope I sealed the flap with a sticker of a bunny carrying a bouquet of flowers. (There are no coincidences!) I had no idea that Ashley was pregnant.

2017 Christmas Gift From Tommy

Mom, Dad, Tommy, Kevin, Gabrielle, Ashley

Chapter 7

The Shark

On April 4, 2009 my husband and I celebrated our 50th Wedding Anniversary by renewing our wedding vows at a Mass concelebrated by the priest who officiated at our wedding on April 4, 1959 and our pastor at Saint Thomas the Apostle Church. Our grandchildren participated in the most meaningful and memorable ceremony. Our children surprised us by inviting family from all over the country and creating a reception that no one will ever forget. Since our family is the most important part of our lives, you can imagine how much that day meant to us.

The gift we gave ourselves was a cruise to the Carribean Islands. While visiting the Island of St. Thomas we went swimming one day at Megan's Bay. My husband was in shallow water while I went in deeper water to swim my laps. All of a sudden I heard "SHARK". Fortunately, I was able to stand in water up to my neck. I looked to my right and sure enough there was a huge shark headed in my direction.

My immediate reaction was that of great pleasure. Its silver fins glistened in the sun as he slowly swam in my direction without a ripple in the water. He was a beautiful sight to behold and I felt a warm sense of peace flowing through my body. My thought was, "His soul could be that fish; after all he loved all creatures great and small. He could be showing off saying, 'Look at me grandma!'."

At the same time, I felt a physical pull from my stomach, pulling me to the fish. I will never forget this experience. I started walking towards the shark. I wanted to be with the shark. In the meantime, I never heard my husband calling to me as he rushed to my side. He jerked my arm, pulling me towards him saying, "What the hell is wrong with you Pat?"

As soon as my husband grabbed me I came out of the mesmerized state I had slipped into. I heard him yelling at me "Are you crazy? Where were you going? What the hell is wrong with you?" I was confused, feeling quite stupid and wondered myself, 'what was I doing'? I could only respond to him, "I'm sorry. You're right, but I felt so peaceful and wanted to be with the shark. I was being pulled to him." We were rushing out of the water, trying not to splash and attract the shark. Strangers on the beach were questioning my foolishness, "Lady, what is wrong with you?" I repeated my response to them, with embarrassment for my actions. When I explained the warm, peaceful feeling going through my body, my husband's response was, "Sure, that was me pissing in the water!". Someone on the beach yelled out, "Lady your husband must really love you. He went into shark-infested water to save you." My husband's response was, "Who's going to cook dinner?" That helped put levity into this serious situation.

The lifeguard said, "The shark was a silver hammer-head shark approximately 10 feet long. They are one of the most ferocious sharks, but will only attack if they are hungry or feel threatened." I am grateful he wasn't hungry. I am convinced my grandson saved my life. Showing up for me that way kept me calm.

When I shared this experience with our daughter Terry she looked up silver hammer-heads. She said, "Mom, you know that feeling of being pulled towards the shark? Well, that was the shark. They have an energy that pulls their prey to them." My theory that Tommy was there that day was confirmed in September of that year.

My husband and I were on Hilton Head Island. I was on the beach reading a book when my husband came onto the beach to give me a gift. He had gone shopping when he left the golf course that afternoon. His gift was a black T-shirt. The print on the shirt was filled with all types of fish. I had a puzzled look on my face as I thanked him for the gift. I thought, "He knows I would never buy this shirt". However, I still thanked him. He said, "Look where your heart would be if you were wearing the shirt!" I looked and was astonished at what I saw......there was a silver hammer-head fish right over my heart!

My eyes filled with tears as I again thanked my husband with deep gratitude for this precious gift. We both believe Tommy drew grandpa's attention to that shirt as his way of saying, "Yes, I was with you in Megan's Bay and I'm here with you now." Grandpa and Tommy were very close. Tommy loved sharing his many interests with Grandpa. Grandpa still chokes up every time he talks about Tommy.

Three months after Tommy died Grandpa had a heart attack. His heart was so broken I was not surprised he ended up with a heart attack. While recovering in the hospital Grandpa had an experience he will never forget. His room was well lit and all of a sudden he saw Tommy in a yellow shirt standing at the foot of his bed. He had forgotten Tommy was dead and was thrilled to see him. Tommy came around to the side of the bed and gave Grandpa a big hug that my husband felt as though he was really present. Grandpa said "I love you Tommy". Then he realized Tommy was no longer here, but he believes Tommy was there to visit Grandpa. He remembers the feeling of that hug! God is good!

Chapter 8

Reflections

Hopefully, by now you can understand why the signs from Tommy are so important. We know we will never see him again in this world, but it is so comforting to experience the many signs that show us he is connected to us in a spiritual way. For me it is my religious beliefs that fuel my experiences. God loves us so much that He suffered on the cross in order for us to have life everlasting. His love knows no bounds; it is so unconditional! His light (which is love) always shines for us, on us, and in us.

I know these signs come from God's love which comes through our loved ones. The more signs I get, the more keep coming. Let me clarify something to you. I do not search for the signs. In the beginning of his death, yes I did. However, once I received these gifts I stopped looking, because I was assured that he was where I believed he was; in the arms of our Lord, and clearly being taken care of by Mary, Jesus' Mom, our Blessed Mother.

I said earlier in this book that I believe Tommy's job in heaven is to greet all the animals that cross over the Rainbow Bridge. However, due to the obvious power he has, I can only imagine what God has him doing. Surely, as far as this earth goes, he has had a tremendous impact on all that knew him here. We certainly know the expansion of the Animal Shelter that he supported will accommodate many more animals and (for the first time) there will be a surgical unit at that facility.

There is a star in Tommy's name in the constellation of Ursa Major. I was not surprised when I heard his star is in The Big Bear. After all, he loved all animals. The next time you look up to the stars please tell Tommy, "Grandma says Hi!"

When I brought my manuscript to my son Tom and his wife Maria to review what I had written about them, we had an experience I will share with you now. When I arrived they had started watching a TV show about the Staten Island events of the day. Lo and behold, on the screen the Deputy Borough President Ed Burke was being interviewed about his concerns with the island's environment. My son taped the show so they could watch it at a later date. The TV remained on with the volume down.

The three of us went into the next room to review my manuscript. As soon as I laid my script out on the table, my daughter-in-law jumped up saying, "Tommy, Tommy! There's Tommy on the TV." We ran to the TV, my son raised the volume and we listened to Ed Burke talking with pride about Tommy. He had a large poster picture of Tommy in the creek at Earth Camp and was sharing Tommy's story and his love for the environment and all animals great and small.

We have met with Ed Burke many times and feel a great kinship with him. It turns out pictures of Ed as a child look very much like Tommy. They shared the same love for nature and had many of the same stories. He shared Tommy's excursion to the Nature Conservancy when he met Atka the wolf. It turned out Ed was in the audience with his family that same day before we ever met Ed.

Before Atka the wolf was introduced to the audience, everyone was told to stay still, not make any noises or reach out into the aisle as Atka walked the aisle for them to see him up close. When Atka came down the aisle he walked over to Tommy who was thrilled with joy. When the event was over Tommy wanted to come to our house to tell Grandpa about "the best day of his life". He was so proud Atka came to him, yet that didn't surprise us. His love for wolves was deep.

In "Spirit's of the Earth", Bobby Lake-Thom writes "a wolf is a good sign. They are protectors, good hunters, wise, cunning, intelligent, strong, gregarious, courageous and yet mysterious."

As it turned out, in the conservancy that day Borough President Jim Molinaro's secretary, Lillian Lagazza had taken a picture on her phone of Atka coming down the aisle. It remained in her phone for 10 months before she knew it was of any significance. In January, a month following Tommy's death, The Borough President invited Tommy's family to his office to discuss his plans to rebuild the animal shelter in memory of Tommy.

They were all discussing the many stories of Tommy when Maria mentioned the best day of Tommy's life was when he met Atka. Lillian asked when that was and proceeded to take out her phone. She scanned through her pictures and found the picture of the wolf walking towards Tommy.

Back to Tom and Maria's house while listening to Ed Burke sharing this with the media, we sat there in awe! Here we were reviewing my book with these signs and Tommy jumps out of the TV with, "HERE I AM FAMILY AS BIG AS LIFE! What do you think about me now???" Speechless and grateful to God!

When Tom, Maria and I were wrapping up our reactions to my attempts to share our stories, I shared my hopes this book will help others. I thanked them for their input recognizing the intense pain of losing Tommy. My son Tom related a conversation he had with a group of old friends from his childhood shortly after Tommy died. Tom thought about how lucky he was to have had a son for nine years. He realized they did not have any sons.

"In those earlier days", Tom told me, "at times I was grabbing out for anything that could keep me from continuing to fall down into the depths of despair. I have to get out of the would haves and should haves. Instead of cursing out God for taking him, I thank God for nine good years of bonding with a son who loved everything I did and was thirsty to learn it all. The other day I was in the back yard when a humming bird came right up to me. I stayed still. It hovered close to my eye level. I felt Tommy's presence!" That folks is what faith is all about! God is good!

On what would have been Tommy's 11th birthday The South Shore Garden Club along with the Parks and Recreation Dept. planted a tree in Tommy's memory on the grounds of the Conference House. The tree is close to the Russell Pavillion at the water's edge of the park. Grandpa and I loved sitting under Tommy's tree, watching the boats go by on the river and listening to the bird's songs, especially when there was a concert playing on the pavilion. However, the pavilion is under some serious renovations and we cannot go near the tree at this time.

The Russell Pavillion was named in memory of a local resident Almer R. Russell who was killed in action in France in 1918. An Eagle was spotted flying over the groundbreaking ceremony for the new pavillion on April 26, 2018.We await the reconstruction, but are so grateful to the construction workers and staff of the Park's Dept. who take good care of the tree in our absence. They placed a flag at the tree for us.

Tommy's tree has survived many weather disasters that have destroyed many trees in the vicinity. We know Tommy protects it and we feel comforted while there. One very windy day my son Tom was feeling very sad, missing his son terribly. He went to visit the tree after the reconstruction had started. There were heavy winds causing him to walk in a slanted fashion, leaning into the wind. His head was down and the tears were flowing. He spotted a peacock's feather in his path. He was walking on a carpet of many colored fall leaves.

He couldn't understand how he did see a peacock's feather amongst all these leaves. He has never seen a peacock in this park. He felt his son's spirit saying, "I'm still here. I'm still with you Dad." He believed his son sent him that feather. Father and son often went to the plantation where Gabrielle took equestrian riding lessons. While Gabrielle was riding her horse Tommy was off searching and collecting peacock feathers. My son's mood changed before leaving Tommy's tree that day.

Our family has numerous signs from Tommy, but I only printed enough to give my readers an example of the importance of signs. I pray every day for the bereaved. I hope this book has shed some light on your darkness. May each and every one of you find your light through the signs your loved ones send. Remember you need to let go of your anger, resentments and any negativity. It is so important to believe in a Higher Power greater than yourself. It does not matter what faith you follow, you just need to believe! Tom and Maria connect with Tommy's love; NATURE! Open your mind and heart and your light will allow the signs to come. The Serenity Prayer helps with all these suggestions!

Craig, Gavin, Ryan, Tommy, Joseph star gazing

Dad, Tommy, Grandpa

Wolf Illustrated by sister Gabrielle

"The Serenity Prayer"

God grant me the serenity

to accept the things I cannot change.

The courage to change the things I can,

And the wisdom to know the difference!

PEACE BE WITH YOU ALL

ABOUT THE AUTHOR

Patricia Monahan and her husband Tom have seven children and nineteen grandchildren. Pat is expecting her fifth great-grandchild. She loves the times she spend with each and every one of her family members. Pat was a Girl Scout Leader, a Cub Scout Den Mother, a Babe Ruth Baseball Team Mother and actively involved in many church and school activities until she began her career.

She retired after twenty-seven years as a New York State Certified Alcohol-Substance Abuse Counselor. She volunteered for eight years on Wednesdays at a homeless women's shelter. Trained by the Archdiocese of New York as a Bereavement Minister she co-founded the Bereavement Ministry at St. Joseph-St. Thomas Parish on Staten Island, NY in January 2000.

On December 17, 2007 Pat's nine year old grandson, Tommy Monahan perished trying to save his dog Sophie from their house fire. The world she had known ended abruptly. She wrote "To Thee We Do Cry (A Grandmother's Journey Through Grief)" as her way to reach others whose faith may be shattered following the loss of a loved one, as well as her way of keeping Tommy's memory alive.

On April 19, 2018 Pat was a recipient of the Staten Island Advance Women of Achievement Award for her contributions to Staten Island over the years.

In 2019 Pat wrote "Love Never Ends" as her way of reaching out to the bereaved who struggle with the finality of death as well as reaching the skeptics about the signs that our deceased loved ones bring us. Working with the bereaved all these years she realized one of the greatest forms of comfort a bereaved person can get are the signs that bring smiles to our faces, warmth to our hearts, besides tears of gratitude to our eyes.

www.ingramcontent.com/pod-product-compliance
Lightning Source LLC
Chambersburg PA
CBHW030140100526
44592CB00011B/982